Lew Powell's

CAROLINA FOLLIES

A Nose-Tweaking Look
at Life in Our Two Great and Goofy States

DOWN HOME™

Down Home Press
Asheboro, N.C.

To Dannye

Contents

Introduction

Since 1977 I have assembled an annual page of Carolinas mischief for The Charlotte Observer, where I work as a reporter and copy editor.

I stole the idea from Esquire magazine, which draws its renowned Dubious Achievements from all over the world. At first I worried that the Carolinas alone would not generate enough screwball news to merit a full page of prime Observer real estate. Boy, was I naive! Each year, in fact, space considerations force me to turn away dozens of worthy items.

The earnest efforts of our politicians, preachers and other overreachers and underachievers make the Carolinas a satirist's paradise. Not by accident, I have come to believe, did Jim and Tammy Bakker choose to set up shop so near the heart of the two states.

Over the years the Carolinas have faithfully provided me the very best in foibles and foolishness. I'm grateful for the opportunity to share.

Lew Powell

Charlotte

January 1990

Politicos

WOULD YOU WANT YOUR SISTER TO MARRY A LEGISLATOR? During a debate over making Yom Kippur a state holiday, N.C. Rep. Foyle Hightower of Anson County inquired as to whether Mr. Kippur had been a Republican or a Democrat.

WELCOME TO THE AGE OF JOHN 'NO MORE TAXES' SMITH AND WILLIAM 'SEX EDUCATION IS A SECULAR HUMANIST PLOT' JONES: The S.C. House approved a bill to permit candidates to use nicknames on the ballot.

I DON'T CARE WHAT YOU SAY ABOUT ME, JUST MAKE SURE YOU GET MY NAME IN BOLDFACE CAPS IN THE FIRST PARAGRAPH:
A memo to employees ordered that the name of Thomas Rhodes, N.C. secretary of natural resources and community development, appear in every state news release regarding water, land, air, parks, fisheries, wildlife or zoos.

UH, LET ME REPHRASE THAT...
"These words, 'rape, kill, pillage and burn,' were certainly not an expression of my true beliefs or an official Marine Corps slogan." — A Parris Island drill instructor, apologizing to his former recruits for a sign he had sanctioned during basic training.

NOW ABOUT YOUR LETTERHEAD, SENATOR — WHICH DO YOU WANT AT THE TOP, THE STATE SEAL OR 'RAPE, KILL, PILLAGE AND BURN'? S.C. Sen. Ryan Shealy of Lexington proposed a state commission to stem "the steady erosion toward the men becoming wimps."

Ivan Mothershead

WELL, YOU KNOW HOW HARD IT IS TO READ A VOTING RECORD FROM A MOVING CAR: N.C. Rep. Ivan Mothershead of Charlotte said he put his picture on his campaign signs to let voters know he wasn't black.

11

MUST HAVE BEEN A BAD CONNECTION, SAM. WHAT I REALLY TOLD YOU WAS, 'GO ON MEDICATION':

Charlotte mayoral candidate Samuel McClure said he had passed up campaign forums because "I consulted God about those, and He told me to go into meditation."

IF LEE ATWATER HAD BEEN RUNNING HIS CAMPAIGN, POOVEY WOULD HAVE COMPARED HIMSELF TO REAGAN AND CALLED JESUS A COMMUNIST — AND WON:

Ted Poovey of Granite Falls, a retired dairy farmer and plumbing contractor who compared himself to Jesus Christ and called Ronald Reagan a communist, lost his third straight bid for a N.C. congressional seat.

WOULD YOU WANT YOUR SISTER TO MARRY A LEGISLATOR?

Craig Lawing

"The only engineering I know about," Charlotte state senate candidate Craig Lawing told an audience of engineers, "is what we call Afro-engineering."

HEAR THOSE JUNGLE DRUMS? THEY'RE SAYING, 'BACK-PEDAL, BACK-PEDAL, BACK-PEDAL':
"I don't take 'Afro' as meaning racial," Lawing explained later. "I don't take for it to mean black. It could be South African over there, where the white people are."

WELL, MAYBE *HE* CAN EXPLAIN AFRO-ENGINEERING:
William Keyes, a black former Gastonian, was hired as a $390,000-a-year lobbyist for South Africa.

UH-OH, THIS SOUNDS A LITTLE TOO FAMILIAR:

State Rep. Woody Aydlette of Charleston, saying he was "slam fed up" with the Federal Highway Administration, proposed that South Carolina secede.

HOLD THE PICKLES:

State Rep. Al Adams of Raleigh introduced a bill to outlaw artificially equipped flashers.

THEY CALL ME MR. FIX-IT:

Lumberton, N.C., city councilman Glenn Maynor admitted fixing traffic tickets: "This helps me in my area, because people will say, 'I know who to go to to get a ticket fixed now.' "

WOULD YOU WANT YOUR SISTER TO MARRY A LEGISLATOR? When N.C. state senators learned their special license tags were to be changed from "Senate" to "State Senate" – eliminating their opportunity to be mistaken for U.S. Senators – they booed loudly and voted down the change.

...AND LUNG CANCER EVEN MORE FUN: President Carter assured North Carolinians that the federal government's anti-smoking campaign was intended only "to make the smoking of tobacco even more safe than it is today."

YOU CAN'T MISS IT — JUST TAKE THE EXIT RAMP MARKED 'CARPORT':

South Carolina spent $40,000 to pave the driveway of a former highway commissioner.

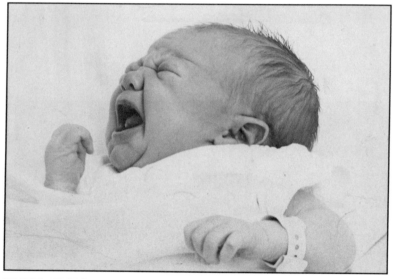

FOR BEST PERFORMANCE BY A PUBLIC OFFICIAL IN A FELONY CASE...

THE ENVELOPE, PLEASE: "Things seem so cold in the newspaper," S.C. State Sen. Joe Holland of Laurens lamented to colleagues in his resignation speech. "When I was indicted (for grand larceny and making a false robbery report), there wasn't a dry eye in the police headquarters. They all love me."

PERSUASIVE NEW EVIDENCE THAT *NOT* SMOKING MARIJUANA MAY CAUSE BRAIN DAMAGE: U.S. Senate candidate Luther Hodges told a University of North Carolina audience he had tried marijuana, then confessed to reporters he really hadn't — he just didn't want to admit it to the students.

MOST CREATIVE ALTERNATIVE TO THE HIGH COST OF POLITICAL ADVERTISING: To attract attention, U.S. Senate candidate Tom Triplett of Chester, S.C., wore one red sock and one blue sock.

I'M SORRY, THE SENATOR CAN'T COME TO THE PHONE RIGHT NOW — HE'S IN THE DEN SWIVELING:

N.C. state senators passed a resolution allowing themselves to buy their chairs to take home.

...AND TO SHOW ITS DEEP APPRECIATION, THE EASTERN BOX TURTLE CHOSE THE N.C. LEGISLATURE AS *ITS* OFFICIAL REPTILE: The N.C. legislature chose the Eastern box turtle as the state's official reptile.

OOPS, A BIT LATE:

A S.C. state senator convicted of racketeering said he was resigning his seat prior to sentencing in order to protect the reputation of the Senate.

GOOD NEWS, GOVERNOR — WE'VE COME UP WITH A WAY TO SATISFY BOTH FACTIONS — AND WE'LL ONLY HAVE TO LEAVE OFF 23 COUNTIES!

Gov. Jim Hunt had to intervene when the printing of 1.1 million N.C. road maps was held up in a squabble between two cabinet secretaries over which officials' names would be listed.

Liston Ramsey

WOULD YOU WANT YOUR SISTER TO MARRY A LEGISLATOR? N.C. Rep.

Charles Beall of Haywood County took the floor to praise the "command presence" shown by the speaker of the House. "Christ had it," said Beall. "Moses had it. Franklin Delano Roosevelt had it. Vince Lombardi had it. Liston Ramsey has it."

'COMMAND PRESENCE' IN ACTION:

"Well," Ramsey greeted a delegation of women lawyers, "what is it you girls don't understand?"

OK, THEN — WOULD YOU CONSENT TO MANDATORY BREATHALYZER TESTS BEFORE VOTING? A S.C. House committee killed a bill that would have outlawed drinking in the State House and Capitol.

BY THE TIME HE TOOK OFFICE, THERE JUST WEREN'T THAT MANY INDUSTRIES LEFT TO DEREGULATE: Gov. Jim Martin accidentally introduced a bill that would have legalized prostitution.

WE'RE DEALIN'! A Union County, N.C., school board member offered to vote to renew the superintendent's contract in exchange for a job for his wife.

IF YOU WON'T GET POLLUTED OFF OUR PRODUCTS, WE WON'T GET POLLUTED OFF YOURS: After Tennessee health officials tightened standards on effluents from the Champion paper mill, State Sen. Dennis Winner of Asheville sponsored a bill to ban Tennessee whiskey.

RECKON YOU'RE NEW IN THESE PARTS, SON, BUT WE DON'T MUCH COTTON TO STRANGERS WRITING 'CA-CA' ON OUR CONESTOGAS: Speaking against obscene bumper stickers, N.C. Sen. Robert Shaw of Guilford County said the pioneers would have tossed aside freedom of speech "if somebody had written four-letter words all over their wagons. There would have been some hangings, ladies and gentlemen."

Jesse Helms

WELL, THAT RETIRES THE TROPHY. WHEN CAN WE RETIRE THE WINNER? For the third time, readers of Washingtonian magazine voted Jesse Helms the nation's worst senator.

...AND IF THEY EVER FIND OUT, THEY'RE REALLY GONNA BE MAD:

"Do you realize there are over 2 million Libertarians in South Carolina?" said Charles Blackwell, state Libertarian Party chairman. "Only they don't know that's what they are."

JUST CURIOUS, JIM — WHAT WOULD YOU HAVE SAID IF YOU *WEREN'T* SO DARN DEFT?

Discussing a proposed NFL stadium, N.C. Sen. Jim Johnson of Cabarrus County said, "I think I can say with some deftness that the major site in North Carolina is either going to be in Cabarrus County or in South Carolina."

THEY SHOULDN'T FEEL BAD — SEN. JOHNSON LIVES RIGHT UP THE ROAD AND HE DOESN'T HAVE A CLUE:

During the debate over financing Charlotte's performing arts center, Rep. Vernon James of Pasquotank County said his constituents "don't know art from nothing. Half of them don't even know what state Charlotte is in."

I KNEW WE HAD A PROBLEM WHEN THE PILOTS' LOUNGE STARTED HANDING OUT 'DESIGNATED FLYER' BUTTONS:

N.C. Sen. Anthony Rand introduced a flying-while-intoxicated bill after receiving reports of Fayetteville pilots requiring helicopters to escort them down.

WOULD YOU WANT YOUR SISTER TO MARRY A LEGISLATOR?

State Senate candidate Jim McDuffie of Charlotte asked elections officials to post signs reminding voters that one of his opponents had died.

Cops and Robbers

BOOK ME, DANNO:

The former police chief of Cornelius, N.C., pleaded guilty to punching the town manager, shooting into Town Hall and stealing a handgun.

AW, GIMME A BREAK, OSHIFER — I WAS JUST DRIVING AROUND 'TIL I SOBERED UP:

A Durham man was charged twice within two hours with driving while impaired. The first time he registered .19 on the Breathalyzer, the second time .16.

DARN POST OFFICE... WHATEVER'S IN THIS PACKAGE, IT'S BROKEN. I CAN HEAR IT RATTLING...

A Morganton man was charged with attempted murder for allegedly mailing a rattlesnake to his former boss.

THAT'S THE FIRST TIME I EVER HAD TO WAKE UP A GUY TO TELL HIM HE HAD THE RIGHT TO REMAIN SILENT: A burglar broke into a Newberry, S.C., convenience store, drank several beers and fell asleep. Deputies arrested him the next morning, after the manager found him dozing behind the counter.

YOU SAY AH-TOME-IC, I SAY AH-TAHM-IC, LET'S CALL THE WHOLE THING OFF: A caller reported a "bum" on the floor, but the York County, S.C., sheriff's dispatcher heard "bomb." That's why eight firefighters, three sheriff's deputies and the emergency preparedness director converged to disarm a transient sleeping in a gas station restroom.

TAKE THESE CHAINS FROM MY TONGUE AND SET ME FREE:

Justifying his reprimand of three officers for talking to council members rather than to their supervisors, Tega Cay, S.C., Police Chief John Short said, "We have a chain of command, and the chain of command is that you go through the chain of command."

HEAR 'EM BANGING THEIR TIN CUPS ON THE TABLE? THAT MEANS THEY WANT THE CHEF TO COME OUT AND TAKE A BOW:

Lee County, S.C., Sheriff Liston Truesdale, considering a switch to more economical TV dinners, said the food he served was so good "People want to get in jail..."

ON THE OTHER HAND, NOW THAT I'VE HAD A CHANCE TO THINK IT OVER, HEY, WHAT'S MY HURRY?

A Charlotte driver who honked impatiently at a slow-moving car got a bullet through his window in return.

31

HE MIGHT HAVE GOTTEN AWAY WITH IT, TOO, IF HE HADN'T PAINTED THAT BULL'S-EYE ON HIS TRUNK LID:

A Greenville, N.C., man was found guilty of insurance fraud after staging at least eight phony traffic accidents, in which he caused other drivers to hit his car.

THAT'S FUNNY — I DON'T REMEMBER THAT MEAT LOAF HAVING TOES:

A radioactive laboratory freezer was stolen from a Chapel Hill loading dock.

YEP, THOSE WERE THE GOOD OLD DAYS, WHEN THE ONLY MIRANDA YOU EVER HEARD OF WORE A FRUIT BASKET ON HER HEAD OR PLAYED SHORT-STOP FOR THE ORIOLES:

"I used to like going up to a house and, if they didn't open the door, just kick it open," recalled longtime Rutherford County, N.C., Sheriff Damon Huskey.

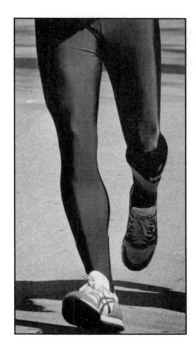

AT LAST — A RUNNER WITH A STORY YOU HAVEN'T ALREADY HEARD 40 TIMES:

A man in a sweatsuit held up a branch bank in Greenville, S.C., then jogged off.

THEY RECOVERED THEM AT A FLEA MARKET, BEING SOLD UNDER THE LABEL 'FREDERICK'S OF MOUNT HOLLY':

Thieves took more than $10,000 worth of bras, panties and girdles from the Bali plant in Gastonia.

THEY CLAIMED THEY WERE ROUNDING UP PROPS FOR A BUD LIGHT COMMERCIAL:

Four persons were charged with trying to steal a pair of blue taxiway lights from Charlotte/Douglas International Airport.

I'D ALWAYS HEARD CRIME DIDN'T PAY, BUT THIS IS RIDICULOUS!

An armed robber took $7.50 from a High Point barber shop, complained that it was too little, handed it back and stalked out.

WE'D BETTER CALL FOR A BACKUP UNIT, CHIEF – I'VE GOT A HUNCH HIS INSPECTION STICKER IS ABOUT TO EXPIRE:

A businessman sued Mecklenburg County police, claiming he had been harassed with nine traffic citations, all dismissed, including driving with unsafe tires and displaying a bent and unreadable license tag.

HEARTWARMING, ISN'T IT, TO KNOW THAT KIND OF OLD-FASHIONED RESPECT FOR PROPERTY STILL EXISTS: A man who stole a Greenville, S.C., patrol car wrote police — from Bismarck, N.D. — that he had managed to removed their decals without marring the finish.

LET'S SEE NOW — 2 JAYWALKERS AT 3 POINTS EACH, 14 BINGO PLAYERS AT 5 POINTS EACH, PLUS A BONUS POINT FOR EACH ONE 65 YEARS OR OLDER... The Greenville, S.C. vice squad held an arrest contest, with the winning team earning a long July 4 weekend.

THE FORCE BE WITH YOU, BUT THE CHIEF BE STEAMED:

Police administrators tried to fire a Charlotte patrolman for allegedly papering the station's walls with Darth Vader posters.

NOW THAT'S WHAT I CALL PASSING A STONE!

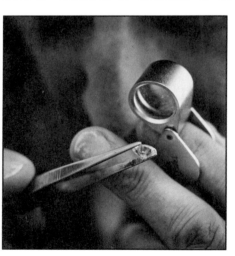

A Westminster, S.C., man was charged with grand larceny after allegedly swallowing a jewelry store's $10,000 diamond ring. Nature brought the ring to light two days later.

WILSON COUNTY, N.C., MAY BE THE ONLY PLACE IN THE WORLD WHERE THE CIVIC CLUBS NEVER HAVE ANY TROUBLE FINDING A PROGRAM CHAIRMAN: The proprietor of a Wilson County brothel testified that Tuesday was Jaycee night, Wednesday was Elks Club night and "and we'd hold Friday for some of the deputies when they came off duty."

ON FRIDAY NIGHT, THERE'S SO MANY GUYS AROUND WITH BADGES ON, YOU CAN'T TELL 'EM APART: The Wilson County sheriff denied accepting bribes from the madam: "She must have me mixed up with someone else."

WORST SOLUTION TO THE PROBLEM OF LOW TEACHER PAY:

Sheriff's deputies arrested a Stanly County, N.C., high school biology teacher after finding 15 marijuana plants growing in a closet beside his classroom and 13 bags of processed marijuana in his briefcase.

MR. MOORE, WE REALLY DO APPRECIATE LOYALTY IN OUR CUSTOMERS. IN YOUR CASE, HOWEVER ...

A robber held up a Charlotte bank, dropped his loot and fled. Ten weeks later he returned. This time he held onto the money but was apprehended before he could leave the building.

EXCLUSIVE! LITTLE GREEN MEN REVEAL CELEBRITY HOROSCOPES!

Two Charlotte police officers won $2,000 each from the National Enquirer for submitting the year's most convincing UFO report.

AND FOR THE *LEAST* CONVINCING REPORT, SEVEN YEARS IN JAIL:

"I was passing by the house and thought I saw a spaceship in the living room..." a Union County, N.C., burglary suspect explained, "so I went inside."

I DON'T UNDER- STAND WHAT WENT WRONG. IT LOOKED SO EASY IN 'BONNIE AND CLYDE': A ski- masked Charleston man stuffed a robbery note into an automatic bank teller. When the machine didn't respond, he shot it twice with a .38 and fled.

NOW, MRS. SCHLAFLY ISN'T ONE TO SAY I TOLD YOU SO, BUT... After 17 years without a prostitution arrest, police in Lancaster, S.C., charged three men who were dressed as women.

ONE FALSE MOVE AND I'LL BLEED ON YOU:

A Bessemer City, N.C., bank robber shot himself in the hand while twirling a pistol on his finger.

THE FAMILY THAT AFFRAYS TOGETHER, PAYS TOGETHER:

An Horry County, S.C., magistrate and four relatives were charged with public fighting at a Democratic precinct meeting.

THEY DIDN'T SUSPECT A THING UNTIL THEY SPOTTED THE JIM DANDY IN THE COLLECTION PLATE: Officials raided a Graham County, N.C., dogfight arena disguised as a church.

DANG. I *KNEW* I SHOULDA SWITCHED TO 'MURDER, SHE WROTE': A Charleston man fled after the woman he was living with spotted him on "America's Most Wanted."

OH, YEAH, ALMOST FORGOT – I COULD USE A COUPLE OF END TABLES, TOO: Police charged a Charlotte man with stealing a rottweiler and threatening to kill it if its owner didn't deliver a couch and a gold chain.

PRAISE THE LORD AND PASS THE SAW:

Authorities discovered three hacksaw blades hidden in the bindings of two Bibles mailed to a prisoner at the jail in Chatham County, N.C.

DO YOU KNOW ME? YOU DON'T? WELL, HOW ABOUT ME? OR...

A man in Winston-Salem was charged with possession of 142 bank cards in 42 different names.

THEY CAN'T DO THIS TO ME, ANDY — WHY, I'D BE THE LAUGHINGSTOCK OF MAYBERRY!

The town of Jefferson, N.C., gave its only police officer a pay cut, demoted him to patrolman, told him to use the town's .38 caliber revolver (instead of his own .357 magnum) and ordered him not to patrol outside town without authorization. He quit.

Jocks

HE LOFTS THE BALL OUT OF THE BUNKER. IT'S ON THE GREEN. IT'S — OOH, OOH, IT'S MY HEART, LAMONT!
Charlotte viewers missed Bob Tway's dramatic winning shot at the 1986 PGA golf tournament when WSOC accidentally switched to a "Sanford and Son" rerun.

YESSIR, RAY, HE'S SOME KINDA TRUCK DRIVER. HE CAME TO DRIVE, ALL RIGHT. LET'S WATCH THAT AGAIN ON INSTANT REPLAY:
In its coverage of the 1980 Bluebonnet Bowl, the Mizlou Network repeatedly referred to "Amos Famous" Lawrence, reported the wrong player of the game for North Carolina and then backed over the game trophies with its camera truck.

OK, LADY, LEMME MAKE SURE I GOT THIS STRAIGHT... YOU WANT THE GOLD SATIN, WITH SHORT SLEEVES. ON THE BACK, IN RED BLOCK LETTERS, 'BUSTER'S 24-HOUR TOWING SERVICE.' AND YOU WANT IT WITH A 47-INCH NECK...

A Cherokee, N.C., woman taught her pig to bowl.

SOME PEOPLE CAN GO TO A COCKTAIL PARTY AND BE PERFECTLY HAPPY WITH A DRINK AND SOME CONVERSATION. NOT MY HUSBAND. OH, NO. MY HUSBAND HAS TO SAY, 'DOES ANYBODY WANT TO SEE A LITTLE PARLOR TRICK?'... AND THEN HE WONDERS WHY NOBODY EVER ASKS US BACK: "As far as I know," said a Catawba County, N.C., sheriff's deputy and karate instructor, "I'm only the second man in North Carolina to lay on a bed of nails and have three concrete blocks busted on my chest with a sledgehammer."

CAPTAIN! OFF STARBOARD! IT'S A GREAT WHITE PRUNE!
Reginald "Moon" Huffstetler of Belmont, N.C., broke a world record by treading water in a Myrtle Beach motel pool for 52 hours, 5 minutes.

HOLD MY CANE, CLARA, I'LL BE RIGHT BACK: An overcoat-clad former East Carolina football coach burst out of the stands in 1977 to tackle the William and Mary quarterback as he scored the winning touchdown. "I'm getting too old for this..." said Jim Johnson, 65. "My wife was really upset with me."

WELL, THAT'S THE LAST TIME I FALL FOR 'ONE SIZE FITS ALL': A Durham Golden Gloves fighter had to retire during the first round because he couldn't keep his cup in his trunks.

IT'S ROCKNE YOU'RE SUPPOSED TO EMULATE, COACH, NOT ROCKY: A Charlotte Pop Warner football coach punched out a player's father after disciplining the boy for not wearing white socks to practice. Meanwhile in South Carolina, two high school football coaches fistfought over the lack of toilet paper in the visitors' dressing room.

IF LIFE WERE A CHEAP SCIENCE-FICTION MOVIE, THIS WOULD BE THE SCENE WHEN THE LAB ASSISTANT SAYS, 'DOCTOR ZOLKOV, WOULD YOU STEP IN HERE A MOMENT? SOMETHING ODD IS HAPPENING WITH THAT SPECIMEN YOU LEFT IN THE PETRI DISH. IT APPEARS — I KNOW THIS IS *IMPOSSIBLE*, OF COURSE — TO BE GROWING...'

Asked about his size 18½ feet, N.C. State basketball player Charles Shackleford noted that "My shoe size seems to go along with my age."

NYET, NYET, NYET! AT THIS RATE, COMRADE EARNHARDTOVICH, YOU DON"T STAND A CHANCE OF GETTING A RIDE FOR THE GLASNOST 300. ONE MORE TIME, REPEAT AFTER ME — 'I BLOWED A TAR... AND GOT SIDEWAYS... BUT THASS RACIN'... I BLOWED A TAR...'

Charlotte Motor Speedway officials proposed building a superspeedway outside Moscow.

THEY'VE GOT THE X'S AND O'S DOWN PAT. IT'S JUST THE OTHER 24 THEY'RE STRUGGLING WITH:

Eight freshmen who entered the University of South Carolina on football scholarships reportedly could barely read and write.

THAT'S TERRIFIC, COACH. UNFORTUNATELY, YOUR PLAYERS...

"At least I can spell it," newly hired USC coach Joe Morrison said about Columbia. "I spent five years learning to spell Chattanooga. Then we moved to Albuquerque."

AND THEIR MATH AIN'T ALL THAT GREAT, EITHER:

"I want to gain 1,500 or 2,000 yards," said USC alumnus George Rogers, sharing his goals for the next NFL season, "whichever comes first."

THREE SMALL STEPS FOR A MAN, ONE GIANT SNORE FOR DONKEYKIND:

Before breaking both legs in a "Death Slide" stunt, dental giant Joe Ponder of Iredell County, N.C., managed to walk up three rungs of a ladder while lifting with his teeth a 500-pound donkey.

THINK UNDERSTAND TONIGHT FOR FIRST TIME AMERICAN EXPRESSION 'MAD AS HORNET':

"This man from Charlotte, he is crazy," said the Lakers' Vlade Divac after the Hornets' Stuart Gray went into a brawling frenzy. "This man from Charlotte, he just kept punching. In Yugoslavia, they have fights but they last only four or five seconds. The man from Charlotte, he kept going."

MAYBE SOMEBODY OUGHT TO INVITE STUART GRAY:

"You like to think that the guys will remember this when they get out on the court," Hornets official Gene Littles said about a pregame devotional service for players. "I'm not saying they won't hit each other, but they might not hit as hard."

NO, NO, HERNANDEZ — I WANTED YOU TO HIT ONE OUT WITH THE *BASES* LOADED:

A Charlotte O's third base- man was suspended for using a cork-filled bat.

IT MUST HAVE BEEN THE FISHNET STOCKINGS. I'M JUST ONE OF THOSE GUYS WHO DON'T LOOK GOOD IN FISHNET STOCKINGS: N.C. triathlete Curt "Ironman" Devereaux lost out to Tina Turner on the "That's Incredible" competition for "Most Incredible Body Over Age 45."

ARE YOU SERIOUS, ED? YOU'RE TELLING ME YOUR DANNY — YOUR LITTLE 6-FOOT-11 DANNY — PLAYS BASKETBALL? Kansas coach Larry Brown hired Ed Manning, a Greensboro truck driver, as an assistant coach. Manning's son, Danny, the state's top college prospect, then transferred to a Lawrence, Kan., high school and signed with Kansas.

Magistrates
and Mouthpieces

NOW THAT'S WHAT I CALL A CHARACTER WITNESS: The defense of a Charlotte businessman charged with money-laundering suffered a setback when his brother-in-law admitted that one of the defendant's favorite expressions was "So I lied."

LORD, GRANT THIS COURT THE WISDOM TO KNOW WHEN AN INNOCENT MAN OF THE CLOTH HAS BEEN RAILROADED ON A TRUMPED-UP CHARGE: A minister awaiting trial for resisting arrest was inadvertently asked to give the opening prayer in an Aiken County, S.C., courtroom.

JUST LOOK AT MY FOREHEAD, YOUR HONOR — SEE WHERE IT SAYS 'GENUINE MOROCCAN LEATHER'? A former parishioner accused Charlotte street evangelist John Cook of banging him in the head with a Bible.

HE'S GOT AN IRONCLAD ALIBI, YOUR HONOR — HE WAS ON HIS WAY TO MOUNT PILOT WITH GOOBER: Greensboro lawyer Louis Allen reported success in invoking the "Mayberry Defense" — likening clients to Sheriff Taylor and other characters from "The Andy Griffith Show."

ORDER IN THE COURT! IF THIS KIND OF FOOLISHNESS CONTINUES, I'M GOING TO CLEAR THE BENCH: A Superior Court judge in Charlotte was accused of sticking out his tongue and blowing a Bronx cheer at the mother of a stabbing victim.

IT'S ALL A MISUNDERSTANDING, YOUR HONOR. MY CLIENT WAS OFFERING HIM A GOOD DEAL ON 1,000 PAIRS OF *LEE*-BOKS:

A federal court in New Bern, N.C., found Yong Han Lee guilty of selling an undercover agent a shipment of counterfeit Reeboks.

WHO SEZ RASSLIN' IS A FAKE? A man was awarded $35,693 after wrestler Wahoo McDaniel allegedly punched him in the nose outside the Greensboro Coliseum.

THE DEFENDANT PLEADS NOT GUILTY, MY HONOR:

A Catawba County, N.C., district court judge, charged with running a stop sign, dismissed the case.

WE FIND THE DEFENDANT GUILTY, YOUR HONOR — BUT HIS ATTORNEY WAS A MILLION LAUGHS:

Despite his lawyer's effort to cast their fight "in the ancient tradition" of Alexander Hamilton and Aaron Burr, an Iron Station, N.C., man was found guilty of maiming a Charlotte man by biting off half his ear.

ZZZZZZ ... ZZZZZZ ... OBJECTION OVERRULED! ... ZZZZZZZZ ...

The city manager of Newberry, S.C., appealed two verdicts because the judge and a juror had allegedly fallen asleep during the trials.

GUILTYGUILTYNOTGUILTYGUILTY NOTGUILTYNOTGUILTYNOTGUILTY ...HOW'M I DOING, BAILIFF?

Mecklenburg County's two traffic court judges had 1,083 cases scheduled on a single day.

... WHILE THE BAND PLAYED 'JAILHOUSE ROCK':

A Greenville, S.C., judge didn't want to disappoint the girlfriend of a 20-year-old man who had just pleaded guilty to cocaine possession, so he allowed him to take her to the prom while under house arrest. "The girl was all upset and couldn't get another date," said the judge.

THEY WERE UN-COVERED, AND SO ARE YOU:

After a Beaufort, S.C., man settled lawsuits filed by three young women he had secretly filmed changing into bathing suits in his house, he sought reimbursement under his homeowners insurance. The company said no, and a court agreed.

OK, JUDGE, MAYBE WE DID RUSH IT A BIT, BUT WE WANTED TO GET HOME IN TIME TO CATCH 'THE PEOPLE'S COURT': A Gaston County, N.C., Superior Court jury returned a not guilty verdict before hearing the defense's case.

AND IF I WEREN'T SO LENIENT, I'D HAVE YOUR WHEELCHAIR TOWED: An Asheville judge jailed a 77-year-old Florida man for parking in the judge's assigned space at the courthouse.

YEAH, BUT IT WAS DEAD LAST IN PLACES FOR RETIREES TO PARK: "Places Rated Almanac" listed Asheville No. 1 in the nation as a place for retirees to live.

BEYOND THE THREE-MARTINI LUNCH:

A federal court fined a Raleigh car dealer $30,000 for deducting as business expenses his maid, his daughter's wedding, his horse feed and his underwear.

FOR A GOOD TIME CALL UNION 76:

When a Charlotte executive saw a name and number on the bathroom wall in his motel, he called the woman, who told him to meet her at a Longview gas station, where he instead encountered her husband and tried to flee but backed his car into another vehicle and then ran into the husband, whom a court later awarded damages of $20,750.

Preachers

WELL, AFTER NECESSITIES, OF COURSE: Less than a month after telling supporters he and Tammy were "giving every penny of our life savings to PTL" Jim Bakker put down $6,000 on a houseboat.

IF YOU CAN'T STAND THE HEAT, STAY OUT OF THE CHOIR LOFT: A Lenoir, N.C., minister was sentenced to 10 years for setting fire to his former church. His lawyer said he had been provoked by, among other things, "unflattering remarks about his wife's singing ability."

WHEN JIM CASTS HIS BREAD UPON THE WATERS, HE NEEDS A LOT OF BREAD AND A LOT OF WATER: In the midst of a 1983 "financial crisis," PTL bought Jim and Tammy Bakker a $375,000 oceanfront condominium.

JIM SAID HE WANTED TO SPEND SOME TIME REFLECTING: PTL then spent $22,000 to install floor-to-ceiling mirrors.

JIM PROMISED HE'D ECONOMIZE BY CUTTING BACK ON THE FRANKIN-CENSE AND MYRRH: New TV dressing rooms for the Bakkers cost $27,000, including gold-plated plumbing fixtures.

C'MON, BIG GUY, YOU'RE PUTTING ME ON! YOU CALL THIS PLACE HEAVEN? I MEAN, IT'S A DUMP! WHERE'S YOUR JACUZZI? AND THAT TACKY BATHROOM — I WOULDN'T WISH IT ON MOTHER TERESA! LOOK, LET ME HAVE TAMMY PUT YOU IN TOUCH WITH OUR DECORATOR IN PALM BEACH... Justifying such expenditures, Bakker asked, "Why should God have junk?"

CHARLOTTE COLISEUM AND AU

BILLY GRAHAM CRUSAD

WRESTLING

ELVIS PRESLEY

ALWAYS THE BRIDES-MAID: U.S. teenagers surveyed by Ladies' Home Journal ranked Charlotte native Billy Graham No. 1 in "achievement in religion," ahead of second-place finisher God.

Billy Graham

GOOD FRIDAY THE 13TH:

Envisioning "heads with eyeballs melting out of their sockets," Jim Bakker revealed his hopes for a hell-like "Lake of Fire" amusement-park attraction at PTL.

PSSSST! TAMMY!... OVER HERE — PORK CHOPS AT 97 CENTS A POUND!

"I take Him shopping with me," Tammy Bakker told PTL viewers. "I say, 'OK, Jesus, help me find a bargain.' "

THE SECOND GREATEST PROJECT WAS 'THE TAMMY BAKKER SHOW':

"This is the greatest project ever in the history of Christianity," Jim Bakker said of PTL's Total Living Center.

**MOST
INVENTIVE
ALTERNATIVE
TO THE
GUN RACK:**
To publicize the
problems of black
youth, an Oxford,
N.C., woman
set out for
Birmingham
strapped to a
cross in the back
of a pickup truck.

**PRAISE THE
LORD AND
PASS THE
PASTE POT:**
Seventeen per-
cent of Billy
Graham's "How
To Be Born
Again" was lifted
virtually intact
from his earlier
book, "World
Aflame."

The Bakkers share with Ted Koppel on 'Nightline'

HEY, JESUS — NEED A LIFT? HOP IN UP HERE WITH ME. YOU OTHER 12 GUYS, GET IN THE BACK: The same year he moved into a $449,000 house in Palm Desert, Calif., Jim Bakker bought a 1953 Rolls-Royce and a 1984 Mercedes-Benz.

WHY, JUST THE OTHER DAY I HEARD JIM SAY HE'D BE JUST AS HAPPY DRIVING AN OL' BENTLEY AS THAT ROLLS: "Jim and Tammy Bakker do not care about material things," insisted PTL executive Richard Dortch.

YEP, THAT WAS PTL, ALL RIGHT:

"They spent nearly two years putting PTL under the microscope," Jim Bakker said of an FCC investigation. "They found nothing."

MAXIMUM GOD:

Tammy Bakker said Hugo reflected God's wrath over "the way the people in Charlotte, N.C., have treated God's people."

WORST IDEA OF THE 1980s:

Before a federal judge sentenced him to 45 years in prison for fraud and conspiracy, Jim Bakker's lawyers proposed he be put on probation, returned to Heritage USA and given five years to fulfill "his vision, his dream and his promise to his partners."

Profs

WHY JOHNNY'S TEACHER CAN'T READ:
Organizers of a conference in Raleigh ripped down a sign with foot-high letters promoting "Excellance in Secondary Education." Explained a N.C. Department of Public Instruction spokesman: "It's awfully difficult to see mistakes in words when the letters are that large."

NOT TONIGHT, MAUDE, I'VE GOT A KLAN MEETING:
University of North Carolina sociologists reported that fears engendered by the 1954 Supreme Court school desegregation ruling may have caused a drop in the birthrate of white Southerners.

YOUR MONEY OR YOUR... AW, THE HECK WITH IT, I THINK I'LL JUST GO HOME AND CHANGE UNDERSHIRTS:

A UNC-Charlotte professor found that assaults, thefts and break-ins decreased during periods of high humidity.

NO MORE GEORGE JONES FOR ME, BARKEEP — I GOTTA DRIVE:

An anthropologist told a Raleigh alcoholism conference that patrons of country-music bars tend to drink faster the slower the song on the jukebox.

SOUTH CAROLINA? OH, YEAH, I REMEMBER NOW — IT'S ON THE WAY TO MYRTLE BEACH, RIGHT?

A survey of N.C. college students' knowledge of geography showed that 5% didn't know North Carolina bordered South Carolina.

OH YEAH? SO HOW COME NOBODY EVER MET ONE OF THESE PEOPLE? According to a UNC journalism poll, almost a third of North Carolinians don't have an opinion on whether Eastern-style barbecue is better than Western-style.

AT LAST — A BARBECUE ISSUE THAT MAKES YOU FORGET EASTERN-STYLE VS. WESTERN-STYLE: State health officials ordered a product recall in 1981 after finding feathers in a bottled barbecue sauce.

YOU AMERICANS HAVE SUCH AMUSING ATTITUDES ABOUT YOUR AUTOMOBILES: A University of South Carolina business professor reported that translation problems plague U.S. companies overseas. "Software" has come out as "underwear," he said, and "car wash" as "car enema."

BRAINS AND THE BEAST:
A UNC study showed ugly men have better educated wives than handsome men.

ONE MORE SCOSH AND SODA, BARTENDER. THEN I GOTTA GO HOME AND HELP MY UGLY HUSHBAND SHTUDY FOR HIS G.E.D.:
Another UNC study showed the more educated a woman is, the more alcohol she is likely to drink.

DIPLOMA FAILS COMPETENCY TEST:
Diplomas for UNC's Class of '75 were recalled when the letters started sliding off.

THERE ISN'T? WELL, DO THEY HAVE A COSMETOLOGY SCHOOL? The newly crowned Miss North Carolina announced that she hoped to attend law school at Princeton. There is no law school at Princeton.

I ALWAYS FORGET — DO MARINATED HATCHBOLTS CALL FOR RED WINE OR WHITE? "The idea isn't as bad as it sounds," insisted a N.C. State professor who predicted edible spaceships.

RESULTS WERE INCONCLUSIVE, HOWEVER, ON MADRAS PANTS: An N.C. State herpetologist discovered polyester leisure suits did not work as a snake repellent.

WAIT A MINUTE, YOUNG MAN — THERE'S BEEN A CRAZY MISTAKE! ACTUALLY, YOU DIDN'T MISS A SINGLE QUESTION!... NOW PUT DOWN THAT WRENCH, WILL YOU? "It's very important how you tell a kid he failed," a Research Triangle education expert said about high-school competency tests. "Some of these kids might... go downstairs and rip out the school's plumbing."

Overreachers and Underachievers

BECAUSE IT WAS THERE:
Less than 24 hours after Gaston,
S.C., dedicated its first stoplight,
a car ran it. Two people were
injured, two cars were totaled
and two others damaged.

**TOPICS SO FAR HAVE INCLUDED
'WHAT'S SO BAD ABOUT
EMPHYSEMA?' AND 'HOW TO
CONFRONT YOUR NONSMOKING
TEENAGER':** Philip Morris began inserting
pro-tobacco editorial messages in packs of
Benson & Hedges cigarettes.

CRUNCH! VROOOM! CRUNCH! VROOOM! CRUNCH! VROOOM! CRUNCH! VROOOM! CRUNCH! VROOOM! CRUNCH!

A woman driving on Charlotte's Independence Boulevard was involved in six rear-end collisions in a period of three minutes.

DANG IT, I KNEW LEE SURRENDERED TOO SOON:

A report showed South Carolina leading the nation in number of nuclear warheads.

ONLY $450, BUT THE BIDET IS EXTRA:

A Winston-Salem inventor introduced the Skitty Witty, a deluxe cat house and litter box available in Cape Cod, Oriental or traditional styling.

YOGI, WE HARDLY KNEW YE:

Nurses at a hospital in Sparta, N.C., were startled to pull back the sheet on a stretcher brought in by the county ambulance squad and find a dead 200-pound bear.

Flat Nose

C'MON, DOC, YOU CAN DO IT — JUST WATCH ED DEMONSTRATE ON JOHNNY: Bandleader Doc Severinsen reneged on his promise to kiss Flat Nose's behind if the dog climbed a pole on the "Tonight Show."

WORST SOLUTION TO THE UNEMPLOYMENT PROBLEM:
With passage of capital punishment, Central Prison in Raleigh received a flood of applications for the $35-a-head job of executioner.

I'M GETTING WORRIED, SKIPPER — IT'S NOT LIKE GILLIGAN TO BE GONE THIS LONG:

Mass murderer Donald "Pee Wee" Gaskins suggested South Carolina could save millions by sending him and other death-row inmates to a deserted island 650 miles from Tahiti.

SEMPER DRY: A Marine Corps band from Parris Island refused to march in a parade in Leominster, Mass., because it had not brought raincoats and didn't want to get its instruments wet.

WHATEVER HAPPENED TO FAKING A STOMACH ACHE?

In a ploy to get out of school, three teenagers in Burke County, N.C., slashed 26 school bus tires.

FORGET THE NOBEL PEACE PRIZE. FORGET THE NATIONAL HOLIDAY. WE'RE TALKING ABOUT 'THE MOST INCREDIBLE BED BARGAIN IN OUR HISTORY!': A Charlotte furniture store commemorated Martin Luther King's birthday with a "King Of A Sale!"

OH, CA-CA:
The principal at Irmo, S.C., High School confiscated 2,700 copies of the student newspaper because a cartoon contained the word "wee-wee."

BUT HIS WORST PROBLEM IS FINDING A FILLING STATION THAT CARRIES 10W-40 EMBALMING FLUID: Police told a Greensboro man he would have to park his metallic blue, four-speed coffin until it was equipped with turn signals and a windshield.

Earl Owensby

PAULINE KAEL HAD A PREVIOUS ENGAGEMENT: A Myrtle Beach moviehouse held an Earl Owensby Film Festival.

WHY, THAT'S MORE BOMBS THAN THEY HAD AT THE EARL OWENSBY FILM FESTIVAL: Investigators reported that enough plutonium to make 18 nuclear bombs was missing from the Savannah River Plant.

IT ONLY HURTS WHEN I SIT ON MY WALLET: N.C. chiropractors signed up for a 10% commission on each mattress they prescribed.

HERE COMES SIMON PETER COTTONTAIL: A front-page caption in the News and Observer of Raleigh referred to Easter as "the day the Christian world celebrates the resurrection of Jesus and the arrival of the Easter Bunny."

WE'RE CALLING IT 'SHEETS': A Ku Klux Klan leader described an exhibit of Klan material at the Forsyth County library as "just like our version of 'Roots.'"

LOOK, NURSE. I DIDN'T COMPLAIN ABOUT THE CATFISH CHOWDER. OR THE FLOUNDERBURGER. OR EVEN THE OYSTER ASPIC. BUT I DRAW THE LINE, BY GOLLY, AT CODFISH UPSIDE-DOWN CAKE!

Craven County, N.C., commissioners voted to fire the hospital administrator after discovering that for the past four years he had been purchasing enough fish to serve every patient twice a day.

YOU DONT HAVE TO BE A WEATHERMAN TO KNOW WHICH WAY THE WIND BLOWS. NOR DO YOU HAVE TO KNOW WHICH WAY THE WIND BLOWS TO BE A WEATHERMAN — JUST SO LONG AS YOU DON'T ADMIT IT: A New Bern, N.C., TV station fired its weatherman for marveling to a reporter that viewers "sit there and listen to me and think I know what I'm talking about... I really think I'm successful with the hoax."

IF ETHEL WANTS A QUART OF BUD AND BUD WANTS A GALLON OF ETHEL, WILL EITHER OF THEM BE ABLE TO TELL THE DIFFERENCE IF YOU GIVE THEM BILLY BEER INSTEAD? A S.C. state study committee recommended banning beer drinking at gas stations.

YOU CALL THAT A MOON SHOT? WHY, YOUR KNEES WERE STILL IN THE CAR:

"We didn't give away albums to everyone who dropped their pants," explained a Concord, N.C., disc jockey who was fired for conducting a "shoot the moon" contest in front of the station. "It had to be a nice shot — really hanging out the car window."

DANG IT, WOMAN, I SAID AU GRATIN, NOT AU NATUREL:

A Salisbury, N.C., man sued his estranged wife for $40,000 after she allegedly threw a pot of boiling grits on him as he stood naked in the bathroom.

WE WANT TO BE THE BEST JAIL IN THE NEIGHBORHOOD:

An Aberdeen, N.C., woman charged with DWI after crashing her car into the county jail told authorities she had mistaken it for a drive-in bank.

I THOUGHT THEY SOUNDED A LITTLE FLAT, BUT MAYBE THAT WAS JUST ME: "I'm sorry I didn't get to see the concert," said a woman who had been shoved over a balcony rail as the Eagles came on stage in Greensboro, "but I heard some of their songs while I was laying on the coliseum floor and waiting for an ambulance."

HEY, JOEY! GET A LOAD OF THOSE BEATITUDES! The Columbus County, N.C., library put the Bible on a list of books available to adults only.

NO ROOM AT THE ASYLUM: A Charlotte new wave band had to change its name after learning that another group was already performing as the Lunatics.

HAD YOU TRIED CAULKING YOUR STORM WINDOWS, MA'AM? A Wilson, N.C., woman arrested for directing downtown traffic in the nude explained that she had been protesting her utility bill.

HAPPY BIRTHDAY TO US, HAPPY BIRTHDAY TO... HEY, WHY ISN'T EVERYBODY SINGING ALONG?

Duke Power charged rate payers for a $300,000 ad campaign congratulating itself on its 75th anniversary.

AND IF YOU COMPLAIN ABOUT IT, WE'LL DELIVER THOSE 100 BABY CHICKS YOU ORDERED IN 1953:

A letter mailed in Providence, R.I., in 1936 arrived in Charlotte in 1981. Because of rate increases during the delivery processes, a postal service spokesman contended, the recipient "actually owes us 15 cents."

SO *THAT'S* WHY THEY CALL IT DEATH VALLEY: A Duke Power map detailing an emergency evacuation plan for the area surrounding the Oconee Nuclear Station inadvertently omitted Clemson.

BUT THEY DID MAKE HIM REMOVE 'THIS SPACE AVAILABLE':

The Raleigh zoning department ruled that a homeowner was not violating sign regulations when he installed a wooden cross, 6 feet tall and set in a 4-foot mound of dirt, in his front yard.

HE SAID HE HAD TO WASH HIS HAIR:

Fifteen robed Klansmen tried to post bond for a black rape suspect in Statesville, N.C. He declined the offer.

I KNEW SOMETHING WAS FUNNY WHEN THE MR. COFFEE PAUSED FOR STATION IDENTIFICATION:

An electronic bug, planted by the principal, was discovered in the faculty lounge at a Montgomery County, N.C., elementary school.

BUT YOU'VE GOT TO ADMIT, THE LIFEGUARD CHAIR WAS AN INSPIRED TOUCH: The Hamlet, N.C., city council ordered 15,000 old tires removed despite the owner's assertion that they constituted a "prototype beach erosion project."

DON'T GO NEAR THE WATER. OR THE TREES. OR THE PICNIC TABLES. OR... A state report found the N.C. parks system so lacking in funding, staffing and maintenance as to pose a threat to public safety.

HOW Y'ALL RUSSKIES SAY 'DOUBLE-WIDE'?
An Albemarle, N.C.,
manufacturer exported
a mobile home to Moscow.

THE LIVERMUSH FOUNDATION HAS ITS EYE ON JULIA CHILD:
The N.C. Yam Commission spent
$15,000 to have its recipes featured on
five installments of "The Richard
Simmons Show."

SALES HAVE REALLY TAKEN OFF SINCE RICHARD SIMMONS MADE SPAM AND YAM SURPRISE:
Carolinians now consume more than 3
million pounds of Spam per year.

YOU FEEL SOMETHIN', NORM?

An angry driver crashed through the wall of a Hickory lounge, injuring his ex-girlfriend and knocking two patrons off their stools.

THE GOOD NEWS IS THE NATIONAL TREND TOWARD SUBTLE RACISM DOESN'T SEEM TO HAVE CAUGHT ON YET IN NORTH AUGUSTA, S.C. THE BAD NEWS IS ...

The owner of the Buffalo Room refused to serve six black officials. "Because they're black," he explained, "that's why."

FOR OUR NEXT NUMBER — OOOF! POW! — WE'RE GOING TO DO A MEDLEY — OUCH! — OF ...

Two rock bands fought onstage at the Greensboro Coliseum for nearly an hour as the crowd looked on and jeered.

PUT AWAY THAT HACK-SAW — AND CHECK OUT OUR LOW, LOW PRICES. DAILY AND  **WEEKLY RATES, MAJOR CREDIT CARDS ACCEPTED:** The former superintendent of the Charlotte Correctional Center was fired after allegations that prisoners had paid officers for leave time.

WITH THIS PISTON RING I THEE WED:

A Wilmington couple married on the starting line of the Southern 500 at the Darlington Raceway.

WITH THIS WING I THEE WED:

A Cabarrus County, N.C., couple said their vows at Kentucky Fried Chicken.

TIMBERRRRR! TIMBERRRRR!
TIMBERRRRR! TIMBERRRRR!
TIMBERRRRR! TIMBERRRRR!
TIMBERRRRR! TIMBERRRRR!
TIMBERRRRR! TIMBERRRRR!
TIMBERRRRR! TIMBERRRRR!
TIMBERRRRR! TIMBERRRRR!
TIMBERRRRR! TIMBERRRRR!
TIMBERRRRR! TIMBERRRRR!
TIMBERRRRR! TIMBERRRRR!
TIMBERRRRR! TIMBERRRRR!
TIMBERRRRR! TIMBERRRRR!
TIMBERRRRR! TIMBERRRRR!
TIMBERRRRR! TIMBERRRRR!
TIMBERRRRR! TIMBERRRRR!
TIMBERRRRR! TIMBERRRRR!
TIMBERRRRR!
THERE! BETTER NOW?

A North Charleston sign company was
fined $36,756 for illegally topping 33
pine trees to give motorists a better
view of a billboard on I-26.

COMING IN ON A WING AND A SNORE:

An air traffic controller at Raleigh-Durham
International Airport fell asleep on duty, forcing
a cargo jet to circle for 15 minutes until he was
awakened.

HECK, I DON'T EVEN STRAP ON MY BULLETPROOF VEST UNTIL THURSDAY: Customers hit the floor when a blaze of errant gunfire shattered windows in a Charlotte convenience store. "On a Friday night you would expect something like this," observed a clerk. "Not on a Tuesday."

GEEZ, YOU DIDN'T TAKE ME SERIOUSLY, DID YOU? Bob Windsor, editor of a pro-Jesse Helms weekly in Chapel Hill, published unsubstantiated sexual slurs against Jim Hunt. "I made no effort to check them out," Windsor explained later, "and do not claim they are the truth or factual in any way."

IT TAKES A LOT OF BRAINS TO MAKE UP FOR ONE BOB WINDSOR: Census figures revealed that Chapel Hill has more college educated residents per capita than any other city in the country.

MOST IMAGINATIVE ALTERNATIVE TO WRITING YOUR CONGRESSMAN:

A Charlotte feminist was arrested at the Cape Cod National Seashore while riding shirtless on a horse to protest anti-nudity regulations.

CHARLOTTE'S LOOKING FOR A DISTINCTIVE IMAGE, RIGHT? WE THINK (KAFF-KAFF) WE'VE FOUND IT:

Environmental scientists rated Charlotte's air the most polluted in the Southeast.

PODNUH, I'M GONNA COUNT TO THREE, REAL SLOW-LIKE, AND IF YOU AIN'T FLUSHED BY THEN...

A North Charleston man accidentally shot himself in the foot while considering turning the gun on his stopped-up toilet.

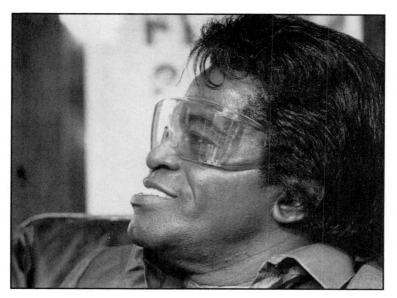

James Brown

BUT WHAT GOT YOU IN TROUBLE, JAMES, WAS WHEN YOU OUTDID CURLY, LARRY AND MOE: "It's hard to believe," complained inmate James Brown, "that when a man outdoes Beethoven, Bach and Brahms they don't have a place for him."

SAY IT LOUD — I'M HERB, I'M PROUD: Herbert Paul Schenck of Westfield, N.C., started an organization to protest Burger King's negative portrayal of people named Herb.

SURE, THE GIRLS ALL GET PRETTIER AT CLOSING TIME — BUT THIS IS RIDICULOUS: The N.C. pork industry was hit with an outbreak of herpes.

THE ONLY THING THAT'S GOT ME STUMPED IS HOW TO KEEP THE HAMBURGER FROM THAWING: A Monroe race fan rigged a freezer box as an infield outhouse. "We put a little disinfectant in there," he said, "and it's not bad at all."

SIGN UP WITH US TODAY, SON, AND WE CAN GUARANTEE YOU A PARACHUTE THAT'LL WORK EVERY TIME YOU JUMP... WELL, ALMOST EVERY TIME: A Fort Bragg soldier who had survived a parachute failure turned down an interview request, because "The captain told me it looks bad for the Army to have stories in the newspapers about how a chute didn't open. He said it might hurt the 82nd's recruiting."

THAT'S FUNNY, I THOUGHT THEY CALLED IT THE PALMETTO STATE:
A Harvard student broke his own world record by riding a Myrtle Beach roller coaster 110 hours in what he called "a half-hypnotic state."

...AND THE WINNER... FANFARE, PLEASE... IS... MORE FANFARE, PLEASE... The Beach Music Awards in Myrtle Beach were delayed an hour while officials searched for the envelopes containing the winners' names.

KILLS LICE BUT LEAVES EVERY HAIR IN PLACE: Headline in the Spartanburg Herald-Journal: MUCH CONFUSION / ON NEUTRON COMB.

WATCH OUT, BOBBY JOE, HE'S GOT A NEUTRON COMB! Two Lincolnton, N.C., men were wounded in a shooting that began as an argument over one's hairstyle.

INSTEAD OF THE TRADITIONAL TELLTALE CIRCLE, GUYS' WALLETS IN THE '90S WILL BE MARKED BY TRIANGLES, OCTAGONS AND PARALLELOGRAMS: Research Triangle scientists reported developing condoms in a variety of unfamiliar shapes.

YOU THINK *THAT'S* BIG — YOU OUGHTA SEE THE WALLET IT GOES IN: Durham County commissioners blocked a health department plan to launch a condom-shaped hot-air balloon 12 stories high.